EFFECTIVE NETWORKING

Venda Raye-Johnson

A FIFTY-MINUTE™ SERIES BOOK

:50™

Viva Books Private Limited
New Delhi • Mumbai • Chennai • Kolkata • Bangalore • Hyderabad

First Indian Edition 2004
Reprinted 2005

VIVA BOOKS PRIVATE LIMITED

- 4262/3 Ansari Road, Daryaganj, New Delhi 110 002
  E-mail: viva@vivagroupindia.net
- 215-216 New Apollo Estate, 2nd Floor, Mogra Lane, Andheri (E), Mumbai 400 069 E-mail: vivamumbai@vivagroupindia.net
- Jamals Fazal Chambers, 26 Greams Road, Chennai 600 006
  E-mail: vivachennai@vivagroupindia.net
- B-103, Jindal Towers, 21/1A/3 Darga Road, Kolkata 700 017
  E-mail: vivakolkata@vivagroupindia.net
- 7 GF, Sovereign Park Apts., 56-58 K.R. Road, Basavanagudi, Bangalore 560 004 E-mail: vivabangalore@vivagroupindia.net
- 101 & 102, First Floor, Mughal Marg Apartments, Narayanaguda, Hyderabad 500 029 E-mail: vivahyderabad@vivagroupindia.net

Published by arrangement with

Crisp Publications, Inc.
1200 Hamilton Court,
Menlo Park
CA 94025
USA

Credits:
Editor: Tony Hicks
Design and Composition: Interface Studio
Cover Design: Amy Shayne and Fifth Street Design
Artwork: Ralph Mapson

ISBN 81-7649-556-5

Published by Vinod Vasishtha for Viva Books Private Limited, 4262/3 Ansari Road, Daryaganj, New Delhi 110 002 and printed & bound at Raj Press, R-3 Inderpuri, New Delhi-110 012

LEARNING OBJECTIVES FOR:

EFFECTIVE NETWORKING

The objectives for *Effective Networking* are listed below. They have been developed to guide you, the reader, to the core issues covered in this book.

Objectives

❑ **1) To explain the difference between maintenance and advancer goals**

❑ **2) To explain networking skills**

❑ **3) To present job search and leadership skills**

Assessing Your Progress

In addition to the learning objectives, Crisp Learning has developed an **assessment** that covers the fundamental information presented in this book. A twenty-five item, multiple choice/true-false questionnaire allows the reader to evaluate his or her comprehension of the subject matter. An answer sheet with a chart matching the questions to the listed objectives is also available. To learn how to obtain a copy of this assessment, please call **1-800-442-7477** and ask to speak with a Customer Service Representative.

Assessments should not be used in any selection process.

ABOUT THE AUTHOR

Venda Raye-Johnson is a licensed counselor and a nationally certified career counselor in Kansas City, Missouri. She is also a speaker, trainer, and consultant in the areas of career development and interpersonal communications skills. She conducts workshops for corporations, government agencies, military installations, and associations.

CONTENTS

WHAT'S IN IT FOR YOU?

EFFECTIVE NETWORKING is a practical how-to handbook on networking skills and strategies. It is a guide to becoming a "people connector." To assess quickly whether EFFECTIVE NETWORKING can help you, look at the 10 statements below. Write "yes" or "no" beside each statement.

_____ 1. I want to increase my understanding of how to network effectively.

_____ 2. I want to explore the benefits of networking.

_____ 3. I want to analyze a strategic networking structure.

_____ 4. I want to implement my networking goals.

_____ 5. I want to set new networking goals.

_____ 6. I want to improve my general networking skills.

_____ 7. I want to pick up general networking tips that work.

_____ 8. I want to improve my career management skills.

_____ 9. I want to increase my job search skills.

_____ 10. I want to improve my skills in leadership.

If you wrote "yes" to any of these statements, EFFECTIVE NETWORKING will be a good resource book for you.

In particular, EFFECTIVE NETWORKING is a good tool for individuals who are job hunting or changing their careers.

EFFECTIVE NETWORKING takes the mystery out of networking by spelling out the networking strategies, skills, and approaches used by effective networkers.

Good luck!

Venda Raye-Johnson

Venda Raye-Johnson

CHAPTER 1

WHAT NETWORKING IS

WHAT NETWORKING IS

We live in the age of knowledge and change. We are in the middle of a knowledge explosion: there is a doubling of knowledge every 1.5 years. Knowledge is power. The right information, the best resources, and the strongest support are needed to keep focused in the midst of change. Effective networking helps us keep our balance and perspective in a world of change.

Everyone networks. That's not a new thing. From the days of smoke signals to the present age of space satellites, people have shared what they have to meet mutual goals. The first recorded use of the word *network* can be traced back to the sixteenth century and referred to the use of fishing nets. Today, networking still refers to fishing. We are still fishing—for information, for resources, for support.

Techniques for networking are changing to meet the need. We have seen the creation of entire organizations whose primary purpose is to connect people for networking. Colleges, professional associations, and even businesses are now teaching people how to network more effectively.

Networking opportunities are being created in many different ways, such as:

- Mentor/protégé programs
- Coalitions
- Special interest groups
- Quality circles
- Sensitivity trainings
- Power breakfasts and lunches
- Ex-employee alumni groups
- Forums
- Retreats
- Computerized network groups

NETWORKING ENVIRONMENT

All the environments on the preceding page put people in contact with each other for the purpose of sharing and accessing information, resources, and support.

THE IMPORTANCE OF NETWORKING

The greatest leadership skill is the networking skill. Leadership through networking allows you to:

- Be a futurist—look above, across, and below for clues of future change and results.
- Set goals—establish new visions to make use of the new opportunities created by change.
- Empower others—inspire, coach, and serve as a resource for others to actualize their potential.
- Lead—build bridges and alliances to make things happen and achieve goals.

Effective networking is the key to success in the 1990s. Effective networking skills are empowering skills. They enable you to access and share information, resources, and support in a strategic manner that achieves goals and purposes.

REFLECTION

Everyone networks. Some people network more purposefully than others. Some network within their own small circles. Others maximize their extended networks. An effective networker does both. How effective is your networking? Answer these questions in the spaces provided.

Why and when do you generally network?

What are the ways in which you typically network?

With whom do you generally network?

List any networking methods you've heard of but haven't used yourself.

REFLECTION (Continued)

Think back to the last three occasions when you had an opportunity to share information, resources, or support. List each contact person's name and briefly describe the networking occasion. Indicate whether you were concerned with information, resources, or support (or all three). Finally, say briefly what the outcome was. Did you achieve your goal?

Network Contact	Occasion	Information Resources Support	Outcome
(a)			
(b)			
(c)			

Ask yourself these questions about the networking occasions you have just described:

Did I firmly plant in my mind a purpose for this occasion?

(a) ____________ (b) ____________ (c) ____________

Was I satisfied with the outcome of this meeting?

(a) ____________ (b) ____________ (c) ____________

Was my contact satisfied with the outcome?

(a) ____________ (b) ____________ (c) ____________

ESTABLISH NETWORKING GOALS

Effective networking requires goal setting. Effective networkers know where they want to go. And they know how to connect with the people who can help them get there.

Place a check next to the statements that describe your current goals.

My goals are:

☐ To change jobs soon

☐ To make a career change

☐ To increase my knowledge and expertise in my field of work

☐ To have my skills and expertise more visible to others

☐ To generate new business and professional contacts

☐ To make new friends

☐ Other goals: ______________________________

____

There's little point in developing a network without goals. If you don't have goals, your networking efforts can become unproductive and your end results fruitless.

GOALS PROVIDE MEANING AND DIRECTION TO OUR LIVES!

EXERCISE TO TRY

To get a clearer vision of your goals, try the following.

Sit back, close your eyes, and relax. Project yourself five years into the future. Ask yourself these questions. Then write your answers in the spaces provided.

Where are you in five years' time?

___

What are your surroundings like?

___

Who will have breakfast with you?

___

As you prepare for work, what type of clothes will you put on?

___

What is your work environment like?

___

What kinds of people do you greet as you begin your work day?

___

What kinds of projects do you have pending?

___

Who will help you achieve your projects?

___

Did this exercise help you repicture your goals?

Networking goals provide you with a focus for how you will develop and manage your network. These goals must be continually evaluated, modified, and adjusted to new changes and needs.

TWO TYPES OF GOALS

There are two types of goals to look at as you begin planning and mapping out your network: *maintenance goals* and *advancer goals.*

MAINTENANCE GOALS

Maintenance goals help you maintain a sense of balance and stability in your life. In this fast-changing world, maintenance goals are essential for emotional equilibrium. Examples of maintenance goals may be to spend more quality time with your family, to have a night out with close friends once a month, or to call long distance to a relative twice a month. Certain people in your life help you keep that balance.

What are some of the things in your life you want to maintain?

____

What are you doing to maintain these goals?

____

Who are the people who help you maintain these goals?

____

How do they help you maintain these goals?

____

ADVANCER GOALS

Advancer goals motivate you to stretch yourself to new challenges and to develop skills. They keep you motivated and energetic. Examples of advancer goals may be to get your graduate degree, take on more job responsibilities, or start your own business.

What are some of your advancer goals?

____

What strategies have you created for achieving them?

____

Who are some of the key people you will need to have in your network to help you achieve them?

____

ASSESSING YOUR NEEDS

As you clarify your maintenance and advancer goals, you will need to begin assessing your networking needs and the types of people you will need to include in your network.

Keep these basic questions in mind as you prepare your network strategies to help you meet your goals:

WHAT —are my immediate (up to 6 months) maintenance and advancer goals?

____

—are my short-range (up to one year) maintenance and advancer goals?

____

—are my long-range (one year and up) maintenance and advancer goals?

____

WHY —are these goals important to me?

____

—am I committed to these goals?

____

WHO —can I get to help me achieve these goals?

____

—how can they help me accomplish them?

____

WHEN —do I expect to achieve these goals?

____

HOW —will I know when I have achieved them?

____

Once you're clear about your goals, you can begin developing and cultivating your network to help you reach your immediate, short-range, and long-range goals.

> Remember, effective networking requires:
>
> - Establishing goals
> - Analyzing the kinds of help you will need in achieving your goals
> - Building and cultivating your network accordingly

CHAPTER 2

PEOPLE SKILLS FOR NETWORKING

PEOPLE SKILLS FOR EFFECTIVE NETWORKING

How Are Your People Skills?

Critique yourself. Check those statements that apply to you. Circle the statements where you think you need improvement.

- ☐ Under most circumstances, I am not easily intimidated
- ☐ I have no trouble expressing myself
- ☐ I have no trouble asking for help
- ☐ I make it a practice to look for good in others
- ☐ People listen to me
- ☐ People do not find me boring
- ☐ I can readily strike up a conversation with strangers
- ☐ I make a conscious effort to concentrate on what others are saying
- ☐ Others are attracted to me
- ☐ I have skills and knowledge that are valuable to others

Effective networking requires a combination of people skills. There are six people skills vital to strategic networking:

1. Asserting yourself positively
2. Asking good questions
3. Listening with your "third ear"
4. Presenting yourself attractively
5. Being viewed as knowledgeable or skillful in a particular area
6. Showing interest in empowering others

These skills will be discussed further beginning on the next page.

PEOPLE SKILLS (Continued)

1. Asserting Yourself Positively

Fact: More than 70 percent of the general population report experiencing shyness at some point in their careers and lives.

If you find yourself shy, timid, and uptight in certain situations, you are not the only one. Everyone experiences shyness around certain kinds of people or in certain situations. Effective networkers learn the skills to assert themselves in spite of these feelings. Following are some reasons for being assertive. Check the reasons you would like to be more assertive.

- ☐ To strike up conversations with new people
- ☐ To ask for help
- ☐ To offer help
- ☐ To lead others
- ☐ To be more visible
- ☐ To let others know who you are
- ☐ To share your opinions and views

Asserting yourself positively is essential to networking. It is you making the first move to get what you want.

Tips on asserting yourself positively

- Take responsibility for getting what you want
- Don't apologize for asking for help
- Take the initiative in offering help
- Don't compare yourself to others
- Look your best so you can act your best
- Accept rejections as part of being assertive

2. Asking Good Questions

Fact: You generally get what you ask for.

The greater portion of your networking dynamics will come in the form of asking good questions. Good questions will lead to good information and good answers.

The word *question* comes from a Latin word meaning "to search for." The bedrock of effective networking is searching out good information. Good questions help you to search out the people and information you need to meet your goals. Many networkers don't get the type of information, resources, and support they need because they don't ask good questions. Following are some things that good questions achieve. Check those that you'd find helpful.
Good questions:

- ☐ Motivate others to take notice
- ☐ Allow others to see your good thinking skills
- ☐ Give others a clear understanding of what you want from them
- ☐ Help you assist others in clearer thinking by planting new ideas
- ☐ Help you get more good information
- ☐ Give you more control in getting your needs met
- ☐ Help others by providing feedback on what they said
- ☐ Affirm the value of others

PLAN AHEAD FOR GOOD QUESTIONS

PEOPLE SKILLS (Continued)

Tips on asking good questions

- When possible, consider your goals before meetings and interactions. Formulate your questions beforehand.
- Use open-ended questions that start out with "How," "Why," "In what way," to search out more depth of information and to keep conversations going.
- Use more specific questions that start with "Who," "When," "Where," and "What," when you need direct, factual information.

Good questions keep the purpose of your networking in the forefront.

3. Listening with Your "Third Ear"

Fact: Good listeners have good connections. Everyone likes a good listener!

More than 75 percent of your networking will require listening for information and answers. It is active listening, or listening with the "third ear." Listening with the third ear requires listening to the total person. Following are some characteristics of good listeners. Check the ones you feel you need to work on. Good listeners:

☐ Listen to what is spoken and what is not spoken

☐ Listen for cues to feelings and meanings

☐ Demonstrate acceptance and interest in the speaker

☐ Reciprocate with good questions

Tips on listening

- Make a commitment to listen fully. Concentrate on the speaker.
- Watch the speaker's body language for emotions and unspoken meanings.
- Keep an open and accepting mind to what is being stated.
- Listen for topics of mutual interest.
- Give regular feedback through smiling, nodding, eye contact, and asking good questions.

PEOPLE SKILLS (Continued)

4. Presenting Yourself Attractively

Fact: 90 percent of how you present yourself is done visually (only 10 percent is done verbally).

The old saying, "You never have a second chance to make a first impression," is true. First impressions are lasting impressions. Becoming a good networker requires presenting an attractive demeanor. Effective networkers project a demeanor of self-assurance that draws others to them.

Your demeanor conveys how you feel about yourself. In the spaces below, write what you would like to communicate about yourself.

What impression would you like to convey?

____

How do you dress?

____

How do you manage your body?

____

How do you use your voice?

____

How do you use your face?

____

You must decide what type of demeanor you want to project to others.

Tips on presenting yourself attractively

- Make it a practice to "dress for where you want to get to."
- Wear clothes that look best on you and colors that make you feel good.
- Wear hairstyles that are flattering to you.
- Wear (and carry) accessories that communicate your seriousness about your goals and where you want to go.
- "Talk with your face" as well as with your mouth. Make sure the two are congruent.
- Prepare a 30-second introduction of yourself and practice until it sounds smooth and natural.

Effective networkers know the importance of presenting an attractive demeanor. How is your view of yourself fitting in to where you want to go?

5. Being Viewed as Knowledgeable or Skillful

Fact: Effective networkers have niches or areas of excellence.

To be viewed as skillful or proficient in select areas is important for feeling good about yourself. Having a special skill or knowledge will help you to be perceived as attractive and a potential empowerer. This in turn helps you to develop, extend, and maintain your own network as well as to get included into the network of others. Others will want what you have.

You have skills, talent, and abilities to offer. Your expertise or niche might be:

- Becoming an expert in a particular field of knowledge
- Developing a special hobby
- Mastering special job skills
- Speaking or writing well

What do you see as your niche?

____

Tips on being viewed as knowledgeable or skillful

- Identify a skill, knowledge, talent, or ability that you would like to become more proficient in.
- Make a plan for strengthening that area.
- Make a plan on how to gain visibility for this proficiency.
- Share these capabilities to empower others. Word will circulate.

PEOPLE SKILLS (Continued)

6. Showing Interest in Empowering Others

Fact: People like people who like them.

An effective networker has the ability to empower others. Empowering others means displaying genuine interest and a helpful attitude. Networkers who empower others are in a very powerful position to multiply their efforts, build a stronger networking team, and lead others. Most of all, these networkers are meeting the human need to be of value and significance to others.

Tips on being an empowerer

- People generally want to be valued. Show and tell them they are valued.
- Listen to them. Listening is an excellent way to communicate value.

People are more likely to help you when you help to empower them.

RATE YOUR PEOPLE SKILLS

How would you rate yourself in each of these six strategic skill areas? Use the following scale:

3—Always
2—Usually
1—Seldom
0—Never

My People Skills

_____ 1. Asserting myself positively

_____ 2. Asking good questions

_____ 3. Listening with my "third ear"

_____ 4. Presenting myself attractively

_____ 5. Being viewed as knowledgeable or skillful in a particular area

_____ 6. Showing interest in empowering others

Your score:

18–16: Your people skills are excellent.
15–12: Your people skills are growing.
12–10: Your people skills are underdeveloped.
Below 10: You need intense development.

An effective networker is on a continuous self-growth campaign. These six skills will lay the foundation for improving the quality of your relationships in both your personal and your professional life. At the same time, these skills will be the ones you use to maintain and work your network. They are also leadership skills.

CHAPTER 3

HOW NETWORKING WORKS

HOW NETWORKING WORKS

We have seen that the word *network* was first used in the sixteenth century in relation to fishing nets. Today, in our global society, we might better compare a fully operating network to the universe. The universe is made up of many systems within systems, worlds within worlds. Webster's dictionary defines the universe as: "The whole body of things and phenomena observed or postulated; the world of human experience." That's a network! Your "universal network" includes people you know and people they know. *Everybody has a friend who has a friend who has a friend.*

Fact: The whole is greater than the sum of its parts.

A network cannot stand alone any more than a star or a planet can make up a universe. A network is comprised of innumerable people and group systems. Each person in your network ties you into their network until your network ties into countless other networks.

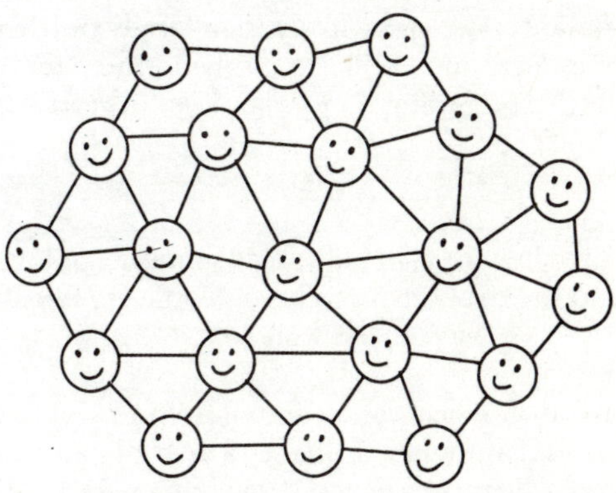

It has been estimated that adults know between 500 and 1,000 people on a social basis. When you multiply each of those 500 to 1,000 persons by the 500 to 1,000 that they know, the numbers become vast.

Most of the 500 to 1,000 people that you know are part of your extended network. They can play a powerful role in helping you achieve your goals.

HOW NETWORKING WORKS (Continued)

Small World

Stanley Milgram reasoned that anyone could reach anyone by linking up with people in their extended networks. In May 1967, he put his theory into operation by asking a sample of people in Massachusetts to use their contacts in reaching a randomly selected group in Nebraska. The results confirmed his theory. The people in Massachusetts were able to reach the randomly selected people in Nebraska within two links. (''Small-world Problem,'' *Psychology Today*, May 1967).

The networking guru, John Naisbett, makes a stronger declaration. He states that he can reach anyone, anywhere in the world, in two contacts!

The Strength of Weak Ties

This power of the extended network is called ''the strength of weak ties.'' This phenomenon has been studied by numerous sociologists. They have found that acquaintances are more likely than family or friends to give individuals direct information and to recommend them for opportunities. (Mark Granovetter, ''The Strength of Weak Ties,'' *American Journal of Sociology*, 8 May 1973).

Acquaintances are people who give only small amounts of time, intimacy, and emotional intensity to the relationship. These people are two or more contacts (or links) away.

These extended network contacts can be important in helping you achieve your goals. It doesn't take vast amounts of time and energy to nurture and cultivate this extended network. Most people you come into contact with will become part of your extended network providing you use the six networking skills covered in Chapter 2.

On the average, people make face-to-face contact with between 15 and 25 people per day. Set goals to increase that average.

TWO COMPONENTS OF AN EFFECTIVE NETWORK

The people in your network influence you in various ways. They may:

- Encourage you
- Listen sympathetically
- Teach you their expertise
- Promote you
- Challenge your thinking
- Inspire you
- Humor you
- Pass on useful information

A few may even become your opponents.

You also influence the people you network with in the same ways.

Your universal network has a central core. This is your network *hub.* You exchange information, resources, and support with the people in this hub—anything from finding a babysitter to getting a promotion!

The hub can be divided into two components: your maintainer network and your advancer network.

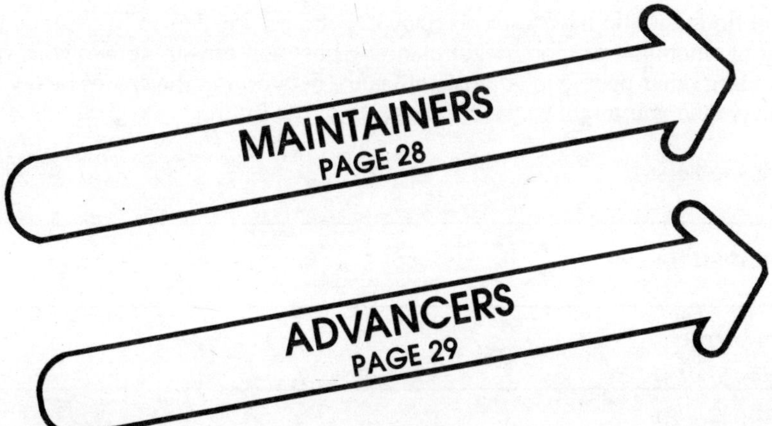

COMPONENTS OF AN EFFECTIVE NETWORK (Continued)

Maintainers

The maintenance component is a small but vital portion of your network. People in your network support your maintenance goals of balance, harmony, and stability. They provide you with support and resources for your emotional needs.

You have four primary emotions out of which other emotions extend. These are feelings of anger, sadness, fear, and joy.

Think in terms of four kinds of maintainers: spirit soothers for anger; spirit cheerers for sadness; spirit boosters for fear; and spirit fillers for joy.

When you are angry and upset, to whom do you turn?

____

When you need a listening ear, to whom do you turn?

____

When you are afraid and hesitant, when you have fears and doubts, who encourages you?

____

When you need a good laugh, to whom do you turn?

____

If you find that you have gaps or if you depend on one person to cover all four areas of emotional support, begin planning how you can strengthen your support by adding other people to your maintenance network. In the spaces below, list some people you might consider turning to in the future.

Spirit soothers:

____

Spirit cheerers:

____

Spirit boosters:

____

Spirit fillers:

____

Advancers

The second component of your network hub is the advancer component. For achieving your goals, consider increasing the number of advancers you have in your network. Advancers are key contacts in helping you advance or move toward your goals, either personally or professionally. You can analyze your advancer component in four dimensions also. Advancers are your role models, mentors, sponsors, and challengers (even opponents).

Role Models

Fact: Everyone has role models, people we emulate consciously or unconsciously.

People who are developing and growing have role models—persons who have qualities, abilities, or styles they admire. Your role models may be people you know or know of. (Always be prepared for the question, "Who are your role models?" in a job interview.) Role models give you a vision of what you want to strive for. Their views and values stimulate you as you move forward to your goals.

Think of people you view as role models—people who have had an affect on where you are now, where you want to be, or how you want to be. What abilities, knowledge, or characteristics do they have that you want to have? (What plans are you making to strengthen your proficiencies in these areas?)

Role Model	Abilities	Knowledge	Characteristics

ADVANCERS (Continued)

Mentors

Fact: Studies show that, on average, successful people have three mentors during their careers. Mentors are people who teach, coach, and advise you in certain areas.

In the past, who has taught you skills or shared expertise or knowledge with you? These skills could be hobbies or business skills.

Mentor	Knowledge	Skills
____________	____________	____________
____________	____________	____________
____________	____________	____________

Sponsors

Fact: It's not just who you know, it's who knows you.

Sponsors are people who serve as your public relations persons. They are your "door openers." Sponsors wield power and influence in recommending you for opportunities. They say positive things about you to others.

Think about instances when you had opportunities presented to you. Who were the people who opened the doors for you and generated these opportunities? Who were the persons who spoke favorably about you in the past? What were the opportunities generated as a result?

Sponsor	Opportunity Generated
____________	____________
____________	____________
____________	____________

In some cases, you may not always know who sponsored you. For that reason, effective networkers routinely use the six people skills covered in Chapter 2. Remember, first impressions are lasting impressions.

Challengers

Fact: Challengers are like oysters. Their rubbing affects bring out the best in you.

Challengers are "devil's advocates." They force you to reconsider your ideas and attitudes. Usually this challenge is against your customary way of thinking. Challengers can sometimes "rub you the wrong way" because you don't always see eye to eye. Challengers are valuable because they stimulate your thinking. They force you to come up with your best.

Whom have you known in the past whose viewpoints frequently differed from yours but whose ideas you later appreciated? Who challenges you to be honest? To defend what you believe?

Challenger	**Idea, Attitude, or Action Challenged**	**Result**

Having challengers in your network hub requires an open mind and an accepting attitude, especially if they are different from you in race, gender, profession, or social status.

> Do you see any gaps or too much overlap in your advancer network? Start working to fill in those gaps. There will always be some overlap—but the less overlap there is, the more powerful and extended your network becomes.

BEING A PART OF OTHERS' NETWORKS

Fact: Those who want friends must show themselves friendly.

An important part of networking is being a link in others' networks. Your usefulness to other people will link you to those people and place you in a position of empowerment. Effective networkers make themselves useful and helpful. *They know that giving power gets power.*

To make yourself useful and helpful to others requires full use of all six networking skills discussed earlier. In particular, the ability to be knowledgeable or expert in some area is critical to strengthening your network.

> The key to cultivating and nurturing your network is sharing your knowledge and/or expertise.

Think about how you can begin making yourself more attractive, useful, and helpful to others. Begin by identifying what skills, abilities, and knowledge you have that you are willing to share. Consider your capabilities in the three areas of character skills, functional skills, and specialized skills.

1. CHARACTER SKILLS

Character skills are "soft" skills because they are nontechnical. They are your personality skills—how you interface with others on an interpersonal level. Descriptions that refer to character skills are such phrases as: "the right chemistry," "good listener," "charismatic," "entertaining." Other character skills include patience, leadership, and being a "team player." Lee Iacocca has said that the main reason why people fail to get ahead is because they cannot get along with other people. In other words, they haven't developed their character skills.

How are your character skills? Answer these questions in the spaces provided:

What kinds of people gravitate to you? Why?

____

____

____

____

In what ways can you be a spirit booster, spirit filler, spirit cheerer, and spirit soother?

____

____

____

____

PART OF OTHERS NETWORKS (Continued)

2. FUNCTIONAL SKILLS

Functional skills are important in many types of environments and on many assignments. Examples of functional skills might include the ability to organize and coordinate projects, write good letters, supervise a staff, and maintain a budget. Key skills are teaching, leading, writing, and speaking.

Write your answers to these questions about your functional skills:

What are some of your favorite functional skills?

____

____

____

In what ways can you mentor, sponsor, or role model for others?

____

____

____

In what ways can you challenge and motivate others to become their best?

____

____

____

FUNCTIONAL SKILLS

3. SPECIALIZED SKILLS

Specialized skills are your ''hard'' skills, or skills of expertise. Examples of these skills might be designing a computer program, training and grooming show dogs, playing a musical instrument, or being highly knowledgeable in African history.

How can you make the best use of your specialized skills? Write your answers in the spaces below.

What persons or groups would you like to share your expertise with?

What functional skills, such as teaching, writing, speaking, or leading, could you use to share your expertise with others?

SPECIALIZED SKILLS

CHAPTER 4

BUILDING AN ADVANCER NETWORK

BUILDING AN ADVANCER NETWORK

In Chapter 1, two types of goals were described: maintenance goals and advancer goals. Maintenance goals help you keep balance and stability in your life. Advancer goals move you forward. Chapter 3 discussed the maintenance and advancer components of a network. The remaining chapters will focus on strategies for building an advancer network.

To begin building an advancer network, organization is required. You will need tools and a system for organizing your networking contact names and telephone numbers and notes on conversations, follow-ups, and future networking activities.

Networking Tools

You will need some type of system to keep track of your contacts. Three-inch by five-inch index cards, spiral notebooks, personal organizers, or a computerized data base will work. Use a tracking system that is comfortable for you. Set up your network file to include the following contact information:

- Name of contact
- Address and telephone number
- How you met this person
- One outstanding point about the person
- Occupation
- Date last contacted
- Conversation summary
- Names of three referrals
- Dates of follow-up on these three referrals
- Date of thank-you letter for the referrals
- Other

SAMPLE NETWORK FILE

A sample network file may look like this:

Telephone and Answering Machine

You'll be surprised at how many contacts will contact you once you've set your network in motion. Time delays and forgotten calls can be avoided by using an answering machine.

Planning Calendar

You need to set time aside to follow through on networking plans. An organizer or pocket planner works well for reviewing and scheduling your daily, weekly, and monthly plans.

Business Cards

Business cards are a must. They reflect your professionalism. Always be prepared for the question, "Do you have a business card?" Whether you are a new college student looking for a job, a business owner looking for sales leads, or just keeping up on your profession, you must have a business card that gives your name, address, and telephone number. Any additional information is your choice. For example, you can include an interest, expertise, place of employment, or company name.

Letterhead and Matching Envelopes

Quality letterhead and matching envelopes show that you are serious about where you are headed. Letterhead with a high cotton content makes a good impression. (Monarch-size letterhead is excellent for both typing or handwriting your thank-you letters or follow-up notes.) Your letterhead can look like this:

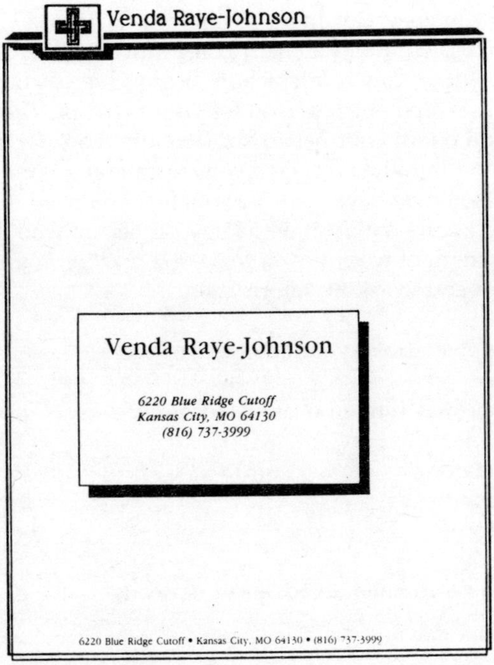

Portfolio or Briefcase

You might consider carrying a portfolio or briefcase for your appointment book, address book, notepad, and any printed materials you'll be handing out or receiving during a networking event. A nice quality carrying case helps you to seem organized and serious about your goals.

Pen and Pencils

Not having a pen or pencil when you need to write down important information can be frustrating. Always carry a pen and pencil in your briefcase or organizer so you won't have to hunt for one at an inopportune time.

THREE WAYS TO BUILD AN ADVANCER NETWORK

Fact: The average person interacts with approximately 20–25 people per day!

To build an advancer network, you will need to begin connecting with more people and to be more goal-focused when interacting with people.

How many people do you generally interact with on a daily basis? Try to increase that number by 20 percent. You may actually come into contact with more than 20–25 people per day. But the key is interaction. Begin to see each person that you are in contact with as a potential person for your network. This may require looking at people in and out of your network differently. Look for positive characteristics. Initiate an introduction. Find some common ground to begin a conversation. That person may have some information you need, or know someone who does, or knows a person who knows a person who does (Review Chapter 3 on ''The strength of weak ties''). Make it a practice to use every opportunity to network and to ask for information.

Why would people help you build your advancer network?

The answer is based on three human relations ideas:

- People like to give advice
- People like recognition
- People like to be helpful

There are three good ways to build an advancer network:

1. **Use your existing network for building your advancer network**
2. **Use organizational meetings, conferences, and such events to meet people**
3. **Contact people directly without the aid of a network contact**

We will look at each individually in more depth beginning on the next page.

1. USING YOUR EXISTING NETWORK

Think about the people in your network hub. See if you can list 200 names. Remember that each of these persons knows between 500 and 1,000 people on a social basis. Multiply those figures together and you have a wealth of network contacts to use.

Don't overlook people like ex-spouses, former students, former teachers, former sisters-in-law, bank managers, insurance agents, the local grocer, workout buddies, hairdressers, local newspaper editors.

Consider who in your existing network can best provide you with the information, resources, or support you need to advance you toward your goals. Ask yourself how each person might best help you. Make a plan to telephone these persons. (A letter is second best.) Prepare a list of good questions to ask before telephoning. A conversation might go something like this:

> Hi, Mike, this is Mary. You may remember me from the Running Club three years ago. I was the person who won last place in the Uphill Competition. Are you still running?
>
> (Mike says he is.)
>
> My purpose for calling, Mike, is to see if you can help me. I am in the process of changing careers. My goal is to become a sports writer. Do you know people who do this kind of writing?
>
> (Mike says he doesn't.)
>
> Do you know of anyone who may know someone who's a sports writer?
>
> (Mike gives the names of two doctors who work in sports medicine at the medical center in town, one of whom had an article published in a popular runners' magazine three months ago.)

Mary is a link closer to getting the kind of information she needs to take her nearer to her goal. The key is contacts. (It takes about two to three network contacts to generate a solid information lead.)

2. USING MEETINGS AND CONFERENCES

The second way to connect with people is through organizational meetings, conferences, and similar events. Consider becoming active in your trade or professional association, civic organizations, or social clubs. Any place where people convene will generate opportunities for you to network. Work on your six basic networking skills at these events.

Evaluate Your Networking Skills

Reflect back to a recent professional or social event you attended. Answer the following 14 questions by writing "yes" or "no" next to each question.

_____ 1. Did you come to the event well groomed?
_____ 2. Did you initiate a conversation with at least 10 people?
_____ 3. Did you introduce yourself using eye contact, a sincere smile, firm handshake, and brief introduction of who you are?
_____ 4. When conversing, did you listen closely for common interests and special needs?
_____ 5. Were you open-minded to persons who may have looked, talked, or acted unlike those you tend to relate to?
_____ 6. Did you actively listen for clues to each person's special strengths and abilities?
_____ 7. Did you genuinely compliment others on their positive attributes?
_____ 8. Did you convey enthusiasm, energy, and direction through your conversation?
_____ 9. Did you let others know your expertise or special skills?
_____ 10. Did you mingle throughout the room?
_____ 11. Did you make a point of introducing any person you talked with to anyone else?
_____ 12. Did you exchange business cards or telephone numbers?
_____ 13. Have you followed up on each significant networking contact with a telephone call or personal note?
_____ 14. Have you since networked your boss or a co-worker with any of your contacts?

Your score:

If you answered "yes" to 12 or more questions, give yourself a "superior" score.

If you answered "yes" to more than 10 but fewer than 12, give yourself an "excellent" score.

If you answered "yes" to fewer than 10 questions, let's get to work!

NETWORKING A ROOM

Here are some guidelines for effectively networking a room.

1. **GO TO THE FUNCTION WITH A GOAL IN MIND.**

   Decide what your networking goals will be for the event. What information or resources are you seeking to help you achieve your goal? Is this a likely event for getting that support? What types of people will be attending such an event? What is the agenda?

2. **PRESENT YOURSELF ATTRACTIVELY.**

   Go confidently. Go prepared. Dress to win. Wear your best colors and an outfit that helps you to feel your best.

3. **TAKE YOUR NETWORKING TOOLS.**

   Take a supply of business cards, a good pen, and a pocket calendar.

4. **DECIDE HOW MANY STRONG CONTACTS YOU WANT TO MAKE FOR THE EVENING.**

   Go for quality of contacts rather than for large numbers. Keep in mind your primary purpose for networking at this event. One or two quality contacts may be a reasonable goal.

5. **ENTER THE ROOM, CENTER YOURSELF, AND OBSERVE.**

   Before getting into conversations with people, take a few seconds to center yourself. Observe the climate of the room. Quickly scan the room, particularly the four corners of the room, where power groups are more likely to form. Mentally decide on one or two people you want to meet.

6. **INITIATE A CONVERSATION.**

   Smile, establish eye contact, extend a handshake, and introduce yourself. The person standing alone will appreciate your rescuing them from a lonely predicament. Initiate a conversation. In his book *Conversationally Speaking* (McGraw-Hill, 1980), Alan Garner states that there are three ways in which you can start a conversation: talking about the situation, talking about yourself, and talking about the other person. This can be done through asking questions, voicing an opinion, or stating a fact. So there are nine possible conversation openings, as shown in the table on the next page.

6. INITIATE A CONVERSATION (CONTINUED).

	About the Situation	About Yourself	About the Other Person
Ask a Question			
Voice an Opinion			
State a Fact			

Imagine you are at a conference or similar function. See if you can think of nine conversation starters—one for each square in the table. Write them in the appropriate squares. Then use them!

7. ASK GOOD QUESTIONS AND LISTEN.

Ask no more than one or two key questions at the beginning. Refine your questions. Rather than asking, ''Can I pick your brain?'' say, ''I need some advice. Can you help me?'' This will generate a more positive response from your contact. Listen carefully to their reply, be willing to hear what they say.

8. CIRCULATE.

Use your discretion as to the amount of time you spend with your contacts at the event. Remember that your goal is to get quality contacts. Be sure to exchange cards as you circulate. At the first opportunity, jot down some interesting points about those persons on the back of their business cards, such as how you met and what you discussed.

9. DON'T GET STUCK.

Don't get drawn into lengthy business discussions at a networking event. Other valuable contacts may be missed. Arrange a follow-up meeting if you want to have a longer discussion. If you find yourself having difficulty in circulating, try these simple strategies: "Here is a person I need to talk with. Will you excuse me?" "Here is a person I need to follow up with. Would you care to be introduced?"

10. FOLLOW UP.

Be patient when you network. Networking is like planting seeds. With care the plants come up—but it takes time. Once you've planted the seeds, you need to water them. In networking it's called follow-up. Schedule follow-up times on your calendar. A follow-up can be a call to say, "I'm thinking about you" or "Did you know. . .?" Or it could be sending your contact a clipping of an interesting article. Clippings of articles will always sit favorably with any network contact. And they help you appear knowledgeable and informed on ideas and events.

THE SECRET TO EFFECTIVE NETWORKING IS FOLLOW-UP.

3. DIRECTLY CONTACTING PEOPLE

The third way to build your network is by contacting people directly, using no network source as a referral. You can get names of new contacts from trade journals and directories. You can also collect names from company brochures, company letterheads, newspapers, or magazines.

Once you have some names, you will need to begin contacting these people. One excellent method for contacting people is called the *informational interview.*

Informational interviewing is useful if you want to break into an established network, extend your specific network hub, or create visibility for yourself. Job-hunters, careerists, sales representatives, and anyone who wants specific information, all use informational interviewing as a networking strategy.

Informational interviewing is *you interviewing your contact* for specific information. In informational interviewing, you have identified a contact who may have the information (and advice) you need to get to where you are going. The informational interviewing approach is virtually threat-free. It is an informal method of asking for information. Nothing more.

Arranging an Informational Interview

Don't be afraid to contact people directly, even if they are complete strangers to you. You are actually paying them a compliment by contacting them. People like to talk about themselves. And remember, everybody likes a good listener.

Arranging an informational interview with someone you've never met might sound something like this:

> Hello, Ms. Brown. My name is Michelle Michels. I read yesterday's article in the *City Magazine* about your program. What you are doing sounds exciting and similar to what I'm doing. It sounds like you and I have some areas of mutual interest here. I've been looking forward to sharing notes with someone having your background. Would it be possible to have lunch with me sometime next week, say on Tuesday or Thursday?

You can use magazine articles, newspapers, or other general publicity to begin targeting people you would like to include in your advancer network.

Here are some other informational interview starters:

> Mr. Jackson, congratulations on your promotion to vice-president at ITS. From the way your background was described in the ———, you were certainly the ideal candidate. Would it be possible to have 15 minutes of your time to talk about an idea I have? My idea is. . .

> Ms. Jones, I am a member of the freelance writers' club. In a recent mailing I received, I noticed that your name appeared on the organization's letterhead indicating that you are a board member and secretary. I think you may be the right person to give me some advice. I'd like to talk with you about an opportunity that I've been offered with XYZ company and get your opinion. Would it be possible for you to have lunch with me on Thursday?''

The interview can be arranged at your contact's office, during lunch, after work, or if necessary it can be conducted over the telephone. The interview should be conducted in a relaxed environment in which you are in control.

SUCCESSFUL INTERVIEWING

The following eight steps will help you make your informational interview a success.

STEP 1. If the appointment is more than five working days away, send a confirmation letter to your contact.

STEP 2. Have a list of good questions prepared ahead of time. Try to ask open-ended questions. It gives your contact more freedom to explore his or her responses, which leads to more information for you. Such questions might be: ''How do you think the director will try to handle this?'' ''In what ways do you feel that taking this promotion will be a benefit to me?'' ''For what reason did you decide not to hire that candidate?''

STEP 3. Listen with the ''third ear'' for additional information about your contact and for relevant information you can share.

STEP 4. At the close of the interview ask for the names of three other persons your contact knows who may be able to provide you with additional information.

STEP 5. If you haven't done so by now, exchange business cards. As soon as time permits, write key bits of information on the back of your contact's business card for future follow-up.

STEP 6. Always, *always,* follow up the meeting with a thank-you letter. Reiterate a particular point of information the contact gave you and tell them that you appreciate the information and the time spent with you.

STEP 7. Record the meeting in your network file.

STEP 8. Keep in contact with this person. A periodic follow-up is the key to tying this person into your advancer network. If you run across an interesting piece of information or a relevant article, call your contact or mail a copy of the article to him or her. This is your turn to give. Schedule times for follow-up and keep a record of your activity.

Interview Preparation

Write your answers in the spaces below.
Which advancer goal do you want to work on?

What information do you need to keep you moving toward that goal?

Who are some local people who might provide you with information or direct you to persons who can help you?

Why do you think these persons may be good contacts for you?

How have you heard of these persons?

Prepare a brief introduction for when you telephone that person. Use some of the suggestions given above.

Summary

When you begin putting your six people skills to work, you will find that you can:

1. Use your existing network to build your advancer network
2. Use organizational meetings, conferences, and such events to meet people
3. Directly contact people without the aid of a network contact

Always keep in mind:

- People like to give advice
- People like recognition
- People like to be helpful

You are actually empowering these persons when you ask for their personal advice, information, and wisdom. When it's done in the right manner, asking for help can be complimentary.

CHAPTER 5

NETWORKING FOR JOB LEADS

NETWORKING FOR JOB LEADS

Fact: Seven out of 10 job leads are found through networking.

If your immediate goal is to find a job, your specific networking goals should be focused on getting job leads. Job hunting is most effective when you are clear on your job goal. The following questions will help you focus on your job goal. Write your answers in the spaces provided.

What skills do you want to use? (Teaching, writing, administrative, etc.).

____

At what level do you want to work? (Management, technical support, secretarial, etc.)

____

In what market do you want to work? (Retail, education, business, industry, entertainment, health care, government, etc.)

____

In what geographical area do you want to work?

____

What salary do you require?

____

Answering these questions will give energy and focus to your networking efforts. When you have decided on your job goal, you can start to plan and organize a networking strategy for job leads.

Networking for job leads depends on three groups of people:

- Who you know
- Who knows you
- Who they know

Networking for job leads is extremely effective because it addresses an important psychological fact: *Employers do not want to hire strangers.*

NETWORKING LEADS TO JOBS (Continued)

In the space below, jot down as many reasons as you can think of for not hiring a stranger.

____

____

____

____

____

____

The opposite of all your statements will be the reasons why network contacts are the best way to generate job leads.

Employers frequently tell others that they are looking for job applicants. Through word-of-mouth, or what frequently is referred to as "the hidden job market," job-seekers and job-givers tie into each other through their networks.

Through networking, a trust factor is established. In other words, "if Mary referred you, then you must be okay." Coming to a prospective employer upon the recommendation of a contact will give you the competitive edge over other candidates. You'll be able to get the better jobs and negotiate for higher salaries.

A 1989 study by the American Association of Counseling and Development (AACD) showed that:

- More than 50 percent of jobs were found through networking, probably a conservative figure.
- Those jobs were frequently higher-paying, higher-status jobs.
- Twenty-five percent of those persons who got jobs through networking stayed longer.
- Better jobs were gotten through acquaintances than through friends.

Think back to your current and past employment. How did you hear about that job opening? The likelihood is that you found out about those positions through talking with friends and acquaintances.

In the space below, write down your last six jobs. Write down how you heard about those jobs: from family members, from friends, from acquaintances, or from some other source.

MY PAST JOB LEADS

Job	Heard about from
____________________	____________________
____________________	____________________
____________________	____________________
____________________	____________________
____________________	____________________
____________________	____________________

If you found that more of your leads came from acquaintances than from family members or friends, that is not uncommon. This is the phenomenon known as the strength of weak ties, discussed in Chapter 3. Acquaintances are more likely to give you direct job lead information and to recommend you to your prospective employers.

THE STRENGTH OF WEAK TIES

Here are some real-life examples of networking through family members and acquaintances.

Leslie, a fashion designer, was looking for a new job. Her husband, Tom, is a computer consultant and business owner. He is very active in community organizations, presiding over several local civic groups. Leslie asked Tom to help her network for job leads.

One day, Leslie came in to see me, frustrated. This is what she said: "Tom's out in the community every day connecting with people. He knows quite a few of the movers and shakers. I keep asking him to make a few telephone calls for me, to make some contacts for me. He's a wonderful husband and excellent businessperson—but he doesn't seem to be actively helping me!"

Regina, a 16-year-old high school junior, caught a city bus to go downtown. She was on her way to the unemployment office to sign up for a summer job. During the 30-minute ride downtown, Regina struck up a conversation with the young lady sitting next to her.

In the course of the conversation, Regina told her that she was on her way to the unemployment office to look for a job. The young lady suggested that Regina try contacting the company where she worked.

Regina contacted the company—and was hired for the summer. She worked that job every summer throughout her remaining high school and college career.

During a job-search skills workshop, seven college students learned about the dynamics of networking. Each student was asked to stand up and request information on a specific job field. One student asked for information on city manager positions. The student sitting across from him smiled and responded: "I can help you with contacts. My father is the city manager at ———."

Never underestimate the value of our extended network hubs. The strength of weak ties can be strength in weakness.

JOGGING YOUR MEMORY

Here are two ways to remember people in your extended network with whom you rarely have contact.

In her book, *21 Steps To A Better Job,* Anita Gates uses the "Favorite & Party Games."

"Twenty Favorites" Game

Brainstorm a list of 20 people who have thought highly of you or of whom you have thought highly. The list below will help you get started.

A favorite friend of your favorite friend

____

A favorite instructor

____

An instructor who favored you

____

A favorite former boss

____

A former boss who favored you

____

A favorite co-worker from a former job

____

A favorite former classmate

____

A favorite business supplier

____

A favorite member of your profession

____

A favorite member of your community

____

Other Favorites:

____
____
____
____
____
____
____
____
____
____
____
____
____
____
____
____

Birthday Party

If you could invite 20 people to help you celebrate your birthday, who would you invite? (Don't include family members and close friends because they will probably come anyway!)

________	________	________	________
________	________	________	________
________	________	________	________
________	________	________	________
________	________	________	________

These lists can be the start of generating job leads. Organize and follow up your leads and contacts with a job-leads sheet like the one on the next page.

JOGGING YOUR MEMORY (Continued)

Job Leads Record

	Name of Contact	Job Lead Given	Date of Follow-up	Result	Date of Thank-you Letter or Phone Call
1.					
2.					
3.					
4.					
5.					
6.					
7.					
8.					
9.					
10.					
11.					
12.					
13.					
14.					
15.					
16.					
17.					
18.					
19.					
20.					

NETWORKING BY TELEPHONE

Networking by telephone can be as effective as meeting people in person, especially when contacting acquaintances. People live busy lives, but they still want to help. If they can help you in 10 minutes over the telephone, they will probably prefer that, rather than meeting you in person for a half-hour.

Here are 10 tips on how to network for job leads over the telephone.

1. Give a brief introduction: who you are, why you are calling, and what help you need.

2. Ask if this is a good time to talk for 10 minutes. If not, ask for a good time to call back. Call back at that time.

3. Ask for their help in sharing with you any information they may know about openings pertinent to your job goals. Good questions can be phrased like this:

   "Do you have any information on job openings in my line of work?"
   "Can you recommend me to someone who might know?"
   "Will you call me back if you hear of such job leads?"
   "Can I be of help to you in some way?"

4. Tell them you don't expect an immediate answer. Ask them if you can call them back at a specific date and time. Usually seven days is a good waiting period. Any longer and your contact may have forgotten.

5. Use a Monarch-size letterhead to hand-write your follow-up letter and enclose a résumé. Remember to include: "How can I help you in return?"

6. Follow up as scheduled. Use your job-leads record to keep track of follow-ups.

NETWORKING BY TELEPHONE (Continued)

7. Whatever information these contacts give, be appreciative.

8. When your contacts give you names of job-lead contacts, ask them if they will call ahead and make a brief introduction of you before you call. (Remember: these are favorite people.) If they don't agree to do this, ask if you can use their name as a referral.

9. Follow up every lead you're given. It's a good idea to write a 30-second script describing who you are and why you are calling. Always use the name of your contact as quickly as possible to establish rapport. A conversation with a lead might go like this:

   You: Hello, Ms. Nelson. Your associate, Sally Smith, referred me to you. My background is in marriage and family counseling. Since your expertise is in mental health, Sally thought you might know of persons who have an interest in individuals with my background.

   Ms. Nelson: If you'd called me last week I could have told you of a position that was open. My friend Jackie Wilson was looking for a therapist for two months. She finally filled the position. But you might try City Health Center anyway.

   You: Thank you. I will. Do you know of other persons who might have an interest in someone with my skills?

   Ms. Nelson: You might try John Smith at Suburban Health Center. Also, you might try Julie Jones. She's in charge of the Association of Family Counselors. She may know of something.

   You: I will, Ms. Nelson. Thank you very much for your help. Do you mind if I call you back and let you know how the leads progressed?

10. Keep in touch. These people can easily become part of your inner network hub—and you may want to be a part of theirs.

VISIBILITY

In job hunting, visibility is vitally important. Visibility is positioning yourself to be seen favorably by people in your network hub who can refer you to job opportunities. Here are some tips on how to be remembered by acquaintances.

- Become active in local organizations. Take on leadership roles. It will place you in centers of influence—places where you are most likely to get sponsored and recommended for opportunities. Consider trade or professional organizations, civic groups, and social and sports organizations. (Remember how to work a room.)

- Volunteer to give presentations in your area of expertise for service organizations and other groups.

- Sponsor others in your volunteer, social, and professional organizations.

- Clip articles and send them to key people in your network as well as to acquaintances who could benefit from this information. It builds goodwill.

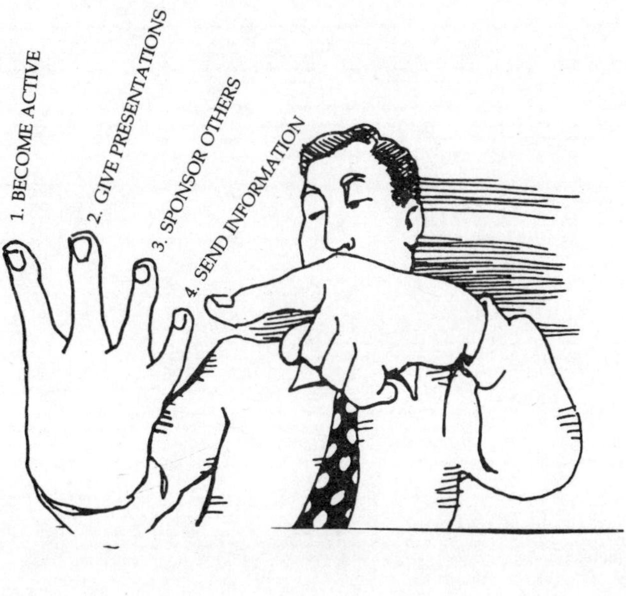

Points to Remember

- Repay every lead with a phone call or a thank-you note.
- Keep in touch. Check in with your contacts every month to let them know how your job hunt is progressing. Keeping visible will generate further job leads.
- Job hunting takes time. Set realistic time goals for yourself. Develop a job strategy plan. Seventy-five percent of your job search plan should be devoted to networking. The key to faster success in your networking efforts will be follow-up. Don't ever underestimate the value of a lead. Develop the art of asking good questions.
- If you are not strategically networking for your job campaign, you are not tapping into the hidden job market.

CHAPTER 6

NETWORKING FOR CAREERING

NETWORKING FOR CAREERING

Fact: Networking is an important part of building a career, because:

1. Most firings could be avoided through strategic networking.
2. Poor career management decisions could be avoided through effective networking.
3. The grapevine has an accuracy rate of more than 75 percent. It is a good source of inside information on organizational happenings.
4. Senior-level managers have, on average, three mentors during their career climb.
5. The higher you go up the corporate ladder, the more important it is to mentor and sponsor others.

CAREER MANAGEMENT QUIZ

Measure how well you are doing in managing your career within your organization. Answer the questions below, writing "yes" or "no" in the spaces provided.

_____ 1. Are you using the grapevine to keep up on events within your organization?

_____ 2. Are you keeping up on the key players in your organization?

_____ 3. Are you networking with key players in related organizations through breakfasts, lunches, or other informal meetings?

_____ 4. Are you generating visibility for your skills and expertise through speaking, teaching, writing, or leading groups?

_____ 5. Are you sponsoring or recommending others for opportunities?

_____ 6. Are you mentoring someone within your organization?

_____ 7. Are you networking with people who are where you want to be in the next 12 months?

_____ 8. Are you networking with people who challenge some of your ideas, values, or beliefs?

_____ 9. Are you using opportunities for visibility in order to acquire a mentor?

_____ 10. Are you networking your boss to key persons outside your organization?

Grade each "yes" answer as one. Your score:
10–9: Excellent careering
8–7: Good
6–5: Needs improvement

To manage your career so as to get to where you want to go, you must network. You need to access organizational information and build a team of supporters. Otherwise, you'll be on the outside looking in.

ORGANIZATIONAL POLITICS

Organizational politics are all around us. Many people naively believe that they can escape "politics" by going into business for themselves or by changing companies. Generally, the work environment changes, but human nature doesn't. Wherever people organize to work together, organizational politics will be involved. Whether you are managing customers, suppliers, volunteers, or even family members, politics are involved. Organizational politics is what people do to influence decisions and to get things done. Politics evolve out of three primary human needs in a group environment:

- The need to be accepted
- The need to be challenged
- The need to be in control

Understanding group dynamics and group skills will help you to handle organizational politics.

Test Yourself

Answer "yes" or "no" to determine if you are influenced by organizational politics.

_____ 1. I would like to have inside information about a new project before my colleagues do.

_____ 2. I take the opportunity to network with "centers of influence" within my organization when possible.

_____ 3. I "bank" favors from work associates.

_____ 4. I attend company socials because it looks good.

_____ 5. I generally dress like my colleagues so that I'll fit into the corporate image.

_____ 6. I would like to have a mentor or sponsor to teach me the unwritten rules in my organization.

_____ 7. I would consider joining the right professional organizations if it would advance my career.

_____ 8. I would like to appear informed on current information within my organization.

> If you answered "yes" to any of the above questions, you are being influenced by or are involved in organizational politics.

BEING IN THE KNOW

Being in the know in your organization is an indispensable career skill.

- It enables you to be seen as attractive and valuable.
- It puts you in positive control.
- It allows you to make more sound decisions and set new goals.
- It helps you to feel accepted and a part of the organization.

Information is the Lifeline of the People in Organizations.

You can get in touch with your lifeline in two ways: through the formal network and through the informal network.

The Formal Network

The formal structure of an organization dispenses information officially. Communication is downward. The formal network dispenses information through such media as:

- Newsletters
- Brochures
- Speeches
- Staff meetings

Write your answers to these questions about your organization.

What is the most frequent means your company uses to dispense information?

___

Is this information "old news" by the time it reaches you?

___

How many other people generally know about this information before it's officially sent out? Who are they?

___

Information gained through the formal structure is reliable. But it's not very effective if it comes to you too late. By the time such information reaches you, people, situations, and events have been long in motion. There may be nothing you can do to make use of the information.

The Informal Network

The informal network is a means of passing on highly accurate information unofficially or off the record. It comes from your cultivated network of mentors, sponsors, challengers, role models, and extended network hubs, as well as from the cultivated networks of other people. The talk about who's getting promoted, who's fallen out of favor with management, what new position is opening up, what competitors are doing—these are all types of information transmitted informally. Informal information is carried on "the grapevine."

The Grapevine

The grapevine is your lifeline. It functions to keep you ahead of official information. It provides you with information early enough so you can be proactive to people, situations, and events before they are set in motion. The grapevine helps you stay ahead of decisions that will affect you. The grapevine carries:

- Gossip—unofficial information
- Rumors—unconfirmed reports
- Perceptions—of how you and others are viewed
- Speculations—on how the situation is sizing up

Although some of it is mere gossip and rumors, as much as 75 percent of the information that trickles through your organization is founded in fact. Sometimes top management deliberately puts information out through the grapevine rather than through formal communications. If you're not nourishing your lifeline, you may be left on the outside looking in.

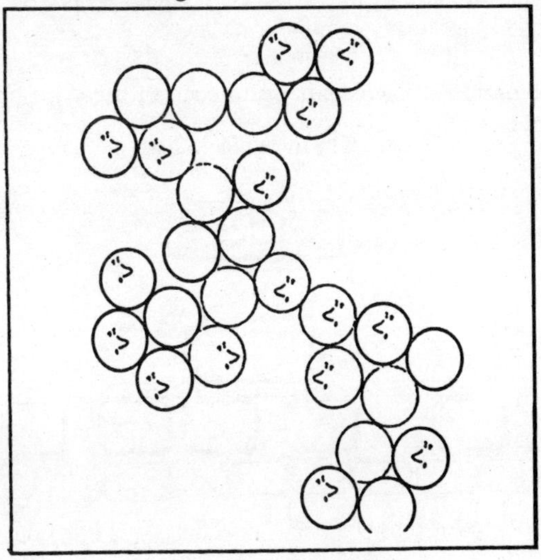

THE GRAPEVINE

THE GRAPEVINE (Continued)

How the Grapevine Works

The grapevine is made up of clusters. Groups of four, five, or six people will usually cluster together during lunches or breaks, at drinking fountains, in the parking lot, or at a favorite restaurant. The grapevine arises out of the tendency for birds of a feather to flock together. Each grapevine cluster has its own set of shared ideas and missions. The members of these groups form alliances based on variations of the notion of "us and them." This "us and them" attitude holds the cluster together. Sometimes the cluster develops an "us against them" attitude.

Here are some examples of clusters:

- Three regional vice presidents meet for lunch at the end of each month to share notes on that month's activities
- Four secretaries meet every day for lunch
- Five employees go biking together
- Six manager trainees meet for a happy hour every Wednesday evening

The Organizational Chart

Look at the organizational chart below. Fill in the names and job titles for your organization or department. (Add boxes to the chart if necessary.)

Color-code those persons who frequently lunch together, take breaks together, or generally appear friendly to one another. Star those groups whose department functions do not require close interaction with each other. The starred groups are the grapevine clusters in your organization.

What common elements or issues surround each of these groups? That will be the strength of that cluster.

Organizational Chart

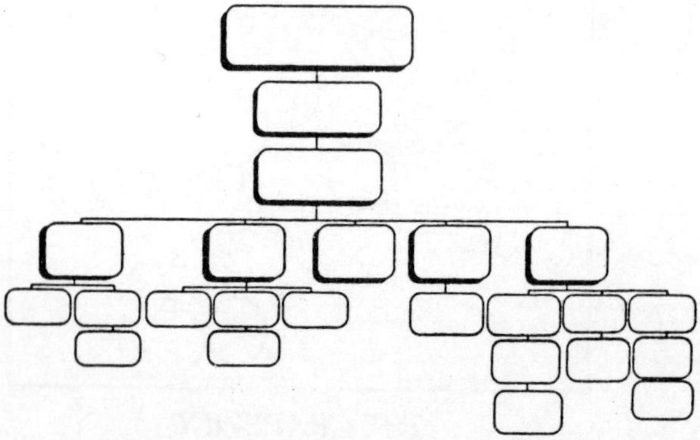

Floaters

Who feeds the grapevine clusters?

Grapevine clusters are nourished through persons known as "floaters." Floaters are like hummingbirds. They float from cluster to cluster, sharing the latest news about organizational happenings and attitudes. They pass on new information from one cluster to another until the entire grapevine has been fed. Floaters move freely between clusters. Their strength is in the fact that they are well perceived and that they feed the clusters.

To stay on top of information in your organization, it is good to know who the floaters are and to build rapport with them. There may be three or four floaters in your organization.

Who are they?

Here are three questions to help you identify the floaters in your organization.

Who is well perceived and makes decisions beyond their authority? (Don't overlook secretaries—they may be the power behind the throne. And don't overlook janitors, mailroom clerks, and other persons low in the official hierarchy.)

____

____

Who knows the latest information before it is formally communicated?

____

____

Who are the persons others go to for advice?

____

____

SIX ORGANIZATIONAL STRATEGIES

1. Be a Floater

One of the best ways to network through the grapevine is to be a floater yourself. In other words, access and share information in the grapevine. As long as the gossip is not personal or malicious, it can build camaraderie and a sense of belonging for the entire group.

Review your six essential people skills in Chapter 2.

2. Get a Mentor

Another popular, informal way to staying in the know about organizational happenings is by getting a mentor. In Homer's *Odyssey,* Mentor was the wise and faithful advisor of Telemachus, whom he taught, coached, counseled, and advised. That's what a mentor does today.

A mentor is not necessarily someone in a high-level position. A mentor can be in a position above you, equal to you, or below you. It is not uncommon to have more than one mentor at the same time. He or she can pass on vital information from the grapevine to you.

Facts to Know about Being Mentored

Selecting a mentor should be done with care. A mentor is an ally. What kinds of people do you want to be associated with? If your mentor falls out of favor with top people in your organization, you may fall out of favor, too. Here are some basic facts about mentoring:

- The mentor relationship generally lasts between two and three years.
- Most successful careerists have, on average, three mentors during their career.
- It becomes more difficult to get a mentor after age 40 or so.
- Mentoring is a give-and-take relationship. You must be favorably perceived and contribute to the relationship.
- Mentoring can be either structured or informal.

How to Get a Mentor

Getting a mentor requires networking for visibility. You must be well perceived by the mentor. If you are seen as up-and-coming, you will stand a good chance of attracting a mentor.

Four high-visibility networking strategies you can use to gain visibility and attract a mentor are:

Write—articles in your area of expertise for trade journals, local newspapers, house organs, and so on.

Speak—As much as possible to trade and professional organizations about your area of expertise. Sign up for your company's speakers' bureau. If you don't have one, start one.

Teach—professional development seminars sponsored by your trade associations. Conduct in-service training in your area of expertise.

Lead—become active on committees and in quality circles and ad hoc groups within your organization. Chairing groups.

Who in your organization is well-perceived and influential?

____

What strategy will you adopt to attract that person as a mentor?

____

____

____

____

SIX ORGANIZATIONAL STRATEGIES (Continued)

3. *Mentor Others*

An often-overlooked means of networking is to mentor someone else. People tend to overlook the value of mentoring as a means of keeping in touch with the lifeblood of the organization. If done right, mentoring can be a win-win situation for you and your protégé. Here are six good reasons why you should consider incorporating mentoring into your networking strategy:

- Mentoring is teaching. Teaching is a way of solidifying what you already know. When you teach someone else, you become the expert.
- Mentoring is a tremendous way of retesting what you have learned. This retesting helps you look at what you know from a new perspective.
- Mentoring can keep you up to date on developments within your field. Protégés who are fresh out of school frequently are on the leading edge of new thoughts, trends, and technology in your field.
- Mentoring is team building. Protégés can one day be in a position to advance your professional growth.
- Mentoring is a way to include a challenger in your network, who will challenge the way you typically think, approach a problem, or handle an assignment.
- Mentoring can be invigorating, revitalizing, and therapeutic. This helps in being well perceived.

Whom do you know in your organization that you would like to mentor?

____

What skills or expertise can you share?

____

Write a brief goal statement about how you can include that person in your network.

____

____

____

____

4. Get Sponsors

A fourth strategy for networking within your organization is to get a sponsor. Sponsors recommend or promote you to others. One may achieve one's goals without mentors, but it's nearly impossible to achieve goals without sponsors. A sponsor can be anyone. The typical sponsor is over the age of 35. Sometimes sponsors become mentors and vice versa. Frequently they can be acquaintances in your extended network, those you seldom come face to face with. You may not always be aware of who has promoted or recommended you. Sometimes your name ''just comes up.'' Visibility and being well perceived is crucial to getting sponsored. The same networking strategies used to get a mentor can be used to get a sponsor. A good networking strategy is to cultivate as many sponsors as possible.

Who are the key players in your organization who have the influence and power to sponsor or promote you?

____

Write a plan to include that person your network.

____

____

____

____

5. Sponsor Others

The fifth strategy is to sponsor others. Sponsoring others places you in a position to be well perceived and influential. Equally important, it allows you to build a team within your own organization. People you sponsor will rally around you, providing you with support, too.

Whom do you know in your organization that you would like to sponsor?

____

Write a short goal statement about how you can include that person in your network.

____

____

____

____

SIX ORGANIZATIONAL STRATEGIES (Continued)

6. Network Your Boss

It's important to get along with your boss. Without the support of your boss, you won't go far. Your boss may be a shooting star and you are hitching a ride. Or your boss may be a jerk and you are trying to live with a difficult situation. In either case, networking with your boss is a good political strategy. In helping your boss strengthen his or her network, you will be strengthening yours, too. Here are some suggestions on how you can network your boss.

- Analyze who are your boss's allies in the organization. Go over the organizational chart and identify the cluster(s) he or she may be a part of. Establish rapport with this cluster. Say favorable things about your boss.

- Mentor your boss. Volunteer to share your skill or specialized knowledge (including avocational knowledge) with your boss. This will place you in a powerful helping position and will encourage respect from your boss.

- Network your boss to key players in outside organizations. If you are networking effectively, you should be connecting with interesting people. Connecting your boss to key players will be a way of promoting good will, increasing your visibility, and being well perceived.

- Sponsor your boss. Recommend your boss for opportunities you think he or she may desire.

BUILDING A NETWORK OF ALLIES AT WORK

Here are some tips on building a network of allies at work—or anywhere else.

- Be helpful and honest to others. Follow the Golden Rule.
- Do favors. Bank some favors . . .
- Then ask for help when you need it.
- Share credit with others.
- Build a niche for yourself by becoming knowledgeable in a certain area.
- Stay close to the grapevine by sharing information as well as accessing it.
- Build a team by sponsoring or mentoring others.
- Continually maintain visibility through teaching, writing, speaking, and leading.

STARTING A FORMAL NETWORK

If you're thinking of starting your own networking organization, here are 10 tips to help you.

1. Research to find out if there is a strong need.
2. Assess the strength of interest in meeting the needs of particular groups of people.
3. Sell the benefits of the network to potential members.
4. Get key leaders to help you lay the foundation and get your network up and running.
5. Establish a meeting format, time, and place for regular meetings.
6. Get names of potential members from your networking sources and mailing lists.
7. Send out announcements using local media.
8. Get letterhead and envelopes, a telephone number, and an answering machine for presenting a professional image.
9. Line up key speakers. Many businesses and nonprofit organizations have speakers' bureaus and will send speakers out free of charge.
10. Set membership fees to cover costs as well as fees for breakfast, luncheon, or dinner—whichever time you are meeting.

The idea for this list was generated by Leslie Smith's article, "Make Networking Your Business" (*Executive Female*, September/October 1987 issue, page 63).

NOTES

NOTES

NOTES

NOTES